Another Poet

Ernest Hartmann

*Best,
Ernest*

Copyright © 2011 Ernest Hartmann

ISBN 978-1-61434-222-9

All rights reserved. No part of this publication may be reproduced, stored in a retrieval system, or transmitted in any form or by any means, electronic, mechanical, recording or otherwise, without the prior written permission of the author.

Printed in the United States of America.

BookLocker.com, Inc.
2011

First Edition

Additional copies of this book can be ordered from the publisher, **BookLocker.com**, or from your favorite online or neighborhood bookstore.

Other books and articles by Ernest Hartmann can be found at: **web.me.com/ernesthartmann** and at **www.tufts.edu/~ehartm01**

To the reader:

You are not a whale, and poems are not minnows to be swallowed hundreds at a gulp. One is enough.

If I have any influence my suggestion would be to read one poem (or at most two or three.) If something happens, if something catches, read it again. Then stop. Come back later. If you find one poem that sings to you, I'll be happy. I have left blank pages here and there to make this style of reading easier.

This book is not an attempt to create a "body of work." Each single poem is wrought slowly, sometimes painfully, best I can. I hope a poem or two may appeal to you. One is enough.

EH

Contents

Another Poet 1

Attraction 2

Mother 4

Evening Song 6

Winslow Street 7

Adam, Falling 10

Life Force 12

Child 14

The Same Wave 15

If Only 16

Evening 18

Still 19

Change 20

Pompeii, April 22

Answer 25

Undefended Clouds 26

Love Is 27

Blue 28

Joan 29

Tiger	30
On the Shore	31
Fools' Gold	34
Unicorn	36
For Ogden	37
He And She	38
Alcohol Helps	39
Echoes	40
History	41
Lullaby ?	42
The Evidence of our Senses	43
January	44
Soon Enough	45
Tonight	46
But Eve	50
Warrior	55
Eyes	60
Arlington 1963	69

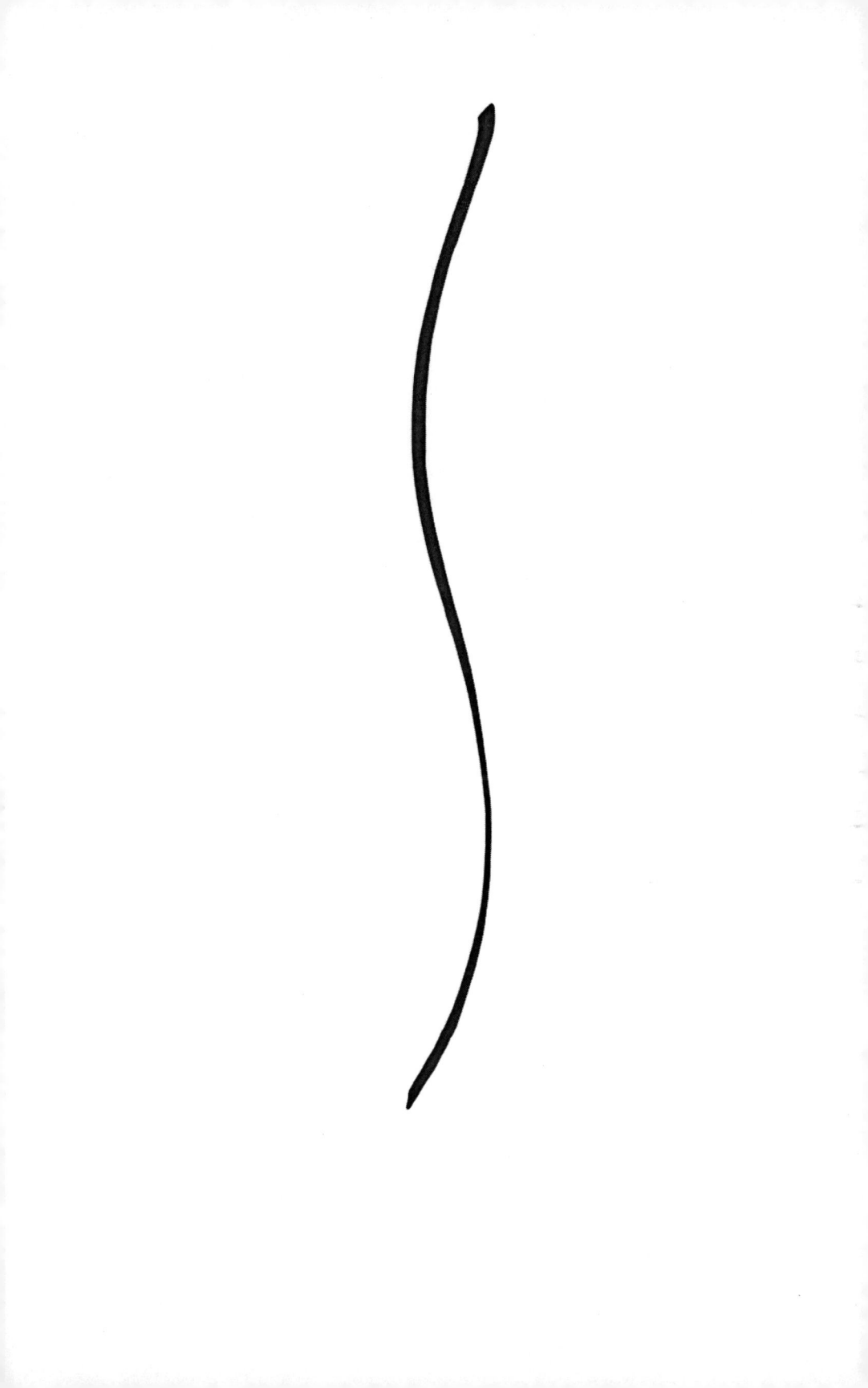

Another Poet

Did the bell ring?

I heard nothing.

At the door, waiting, unhurried,

Stands the final poet.

Stands still and states her syllables,

Not one not necessary.

No practiced drummer of intricate meter she,

No peacock-painter nor crystal palace architect.

Slowly she speaks, and softly.

She beckons me to the purity of her line,

Her poem is a simpler one than mine.

Attraction

(To be spoken on a deck by the seashore)

Sun

Holds earth captive, earth moon, moon sea. You me.

The gravity of attraction

Bends

Our stiff separate tangents

Into one complicity.

The eye does not tire of the sight of the sea.

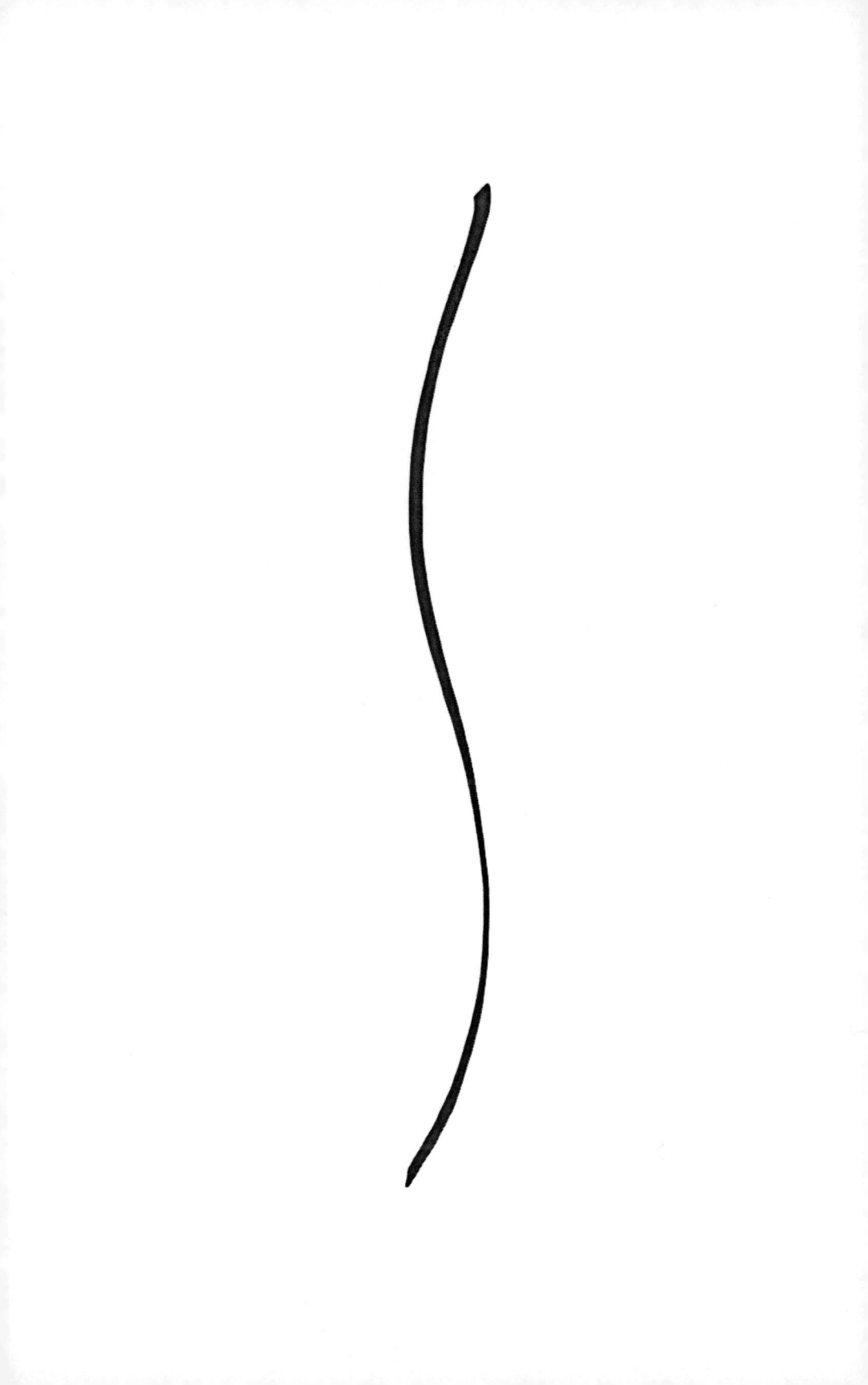

Mother

The lean, perfectly muscled cheetah crouches,

Quiet, aching with her potential speed,

Sees

The herd of elegant impala flying by

Fleet as the wind, not fleet enough she knows.

Sees also

The hyenas grinning in the bush behind her,

Lurking, slow but powerful, awaiting her kill.

Knows

That she will have time, barely,

For a single bite. And with luck

Her kitten beside her will have one bite

Before they come, chase off the lightweight sprinters

And carry off the prize. She'll be hungry still.

What use? What use? She hesitates,

But her kitten, patient at her side,

Still needs to eat, still needs to learn the chase.

Flesh flash, meteor, a streak of fire unstoppable,

She leaps, as was foreseen, as was foretold.

The hyenas play their parts, grow fat and old.

Evening Song

(after Goethe, distantly)

The storm has now subsided, and the light.

The sea is calm.

The single gull that passes here at sunset

Is asleep in its nest.

Nearly dark. Barely moon enough

To wonder. Wait a bit. Soon enough

You too will rest.

Winslow Street

Above the dead on Winslow Street

I tread the steps they trod.

The light is bright, the gull's cry sharp.

I do not hear them quite,

I feel them hearing me.

We travel our separate ways but not

As distant as we used to be.

Along the dead on Winslow Street

My steps still have their way.

I see the sights my hundred fathers saw,

The irregular wounded guys with perfect feet.

Here Robert Lowell had his ups and downs,

And all those Williams of Westminster

Are here on one unbending street.

Vienna, Boston and London are equally near.

My fathers all commingle here.

Among the dead on Winslow Street

My feet are clay to clay.

Among the dead on Winslow Street

Night is not far from day.

The sun is dimmer, the misted land

 Is entangled in ocean, the ocean in sand.

Sylvia , Emily, even Sappho become

My fathers, one by one.

The tides of the earth are slowly rising

As here my steps are done.

Someone's walking there on Winslow Street,

There are no streets but one.

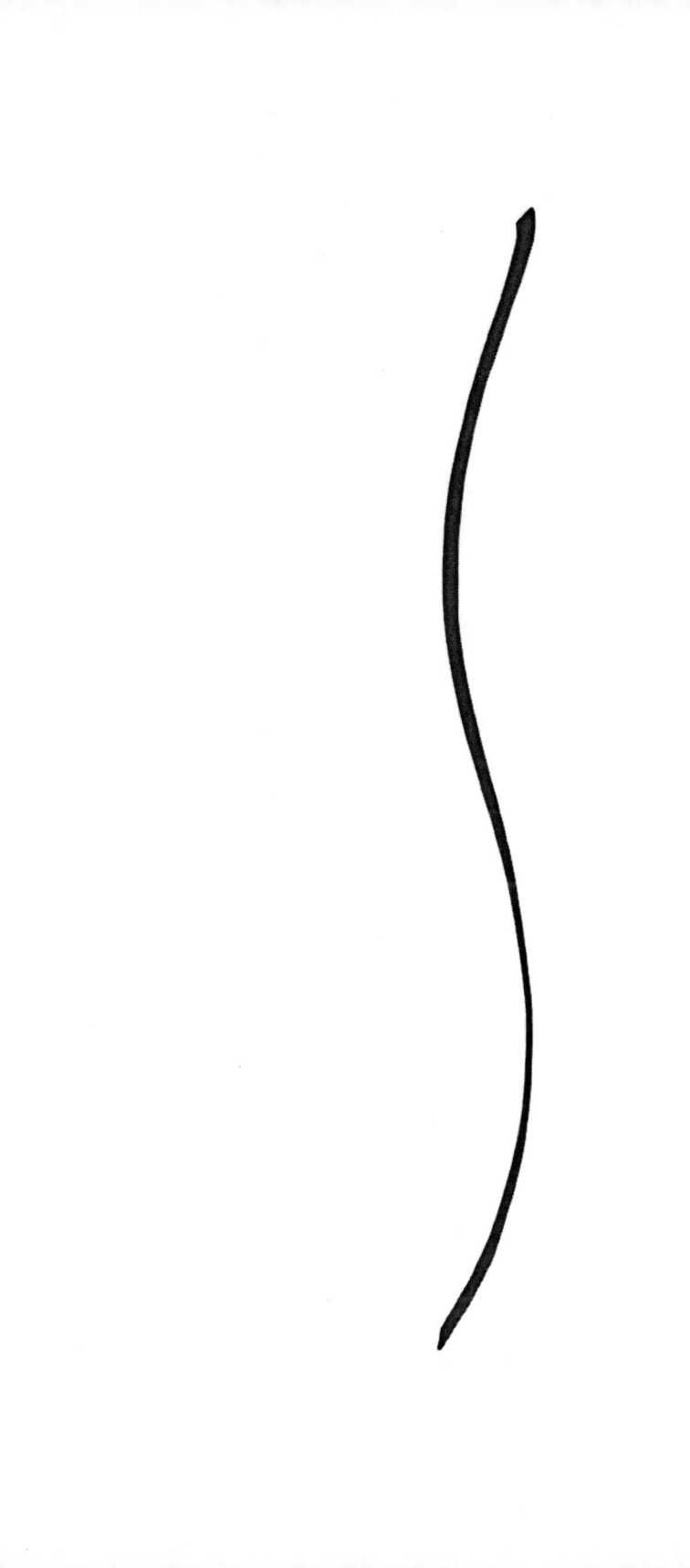

Adam, Falling

No no, that hasn't changed.

Like the he-goat and the she-goat

We'd been fucking all along.

Goat, lion, even the problematic porcupine.

I watched each one so I could name them well.

I knew that she and I were of their kind.

Yet in my body something has been thinned.

The wind blows through me when there is no wind.

No one is near me, yet her face

Slides through the pores of my once solid skin.

Bits of her song bring water to my eyes

As onions do. When she has wandered off

I sudden think – has she now found another?

But no, ridiculous ! Then she returns

And all is as it was before. Except

My words are gone, I cannot speak to tell her

I've lost the solid outline I once had.

I was like stone, am more like water now.

This melting malady is mine alone.

I look about. The goat and lion do not know it.

But nothing else. That's all that's new. That's it.

That's all that's changed since first I bit

Into that sweet prohibited and overperfect fruit.

Life Force

I know this moth,

Watched him an hour ago

Willing his path on the wind.

He is motionless.

Something is changed

I reach out to touch him,

He falls into separate pieces.

Each follows the will of the wind.

Noon. The most brilliant of beach days.

Amid the clash of boom-boxes and beer

I see a woman pulled from the water,

Old, old, her muscles relaxed, too relaxed,

Hideous separate serpents under the ash-blue skin.

An hour ago she was young.

It is warm. A soft cloudy morning.

An hour of calm.

I hold my molecules together.

Are there whispers of love in the wind?

Child

In no sense bystander

Everchild

Play yes and laugh yes and know

All ready all old tales new tales

Helen heaven

Erect collide part destroy

And burning cities far and wide

There never was nor will be ever

A place to hide

The Same Wave

The same wave breaks on every shore.

Every love was loved before.

Is this my love a metaphor?

Never happens happenstance.

I am built of transference.

A newborn dancer in an ancient dance.

If Only

Again, again stutters the October flutterby

To me, there. In flower still. Again to me.

Return again, can any thing again return?

If only. The caterpillar only alters,

Does the flutterby die?

Hope does not know to die.

She. Rerun, she. Finale through to overture.

To me, to me, the reddening leaves revive to green,

Fading blossoms into glowing buds.

If only. Again, once only spring to me.

One clysmic burst of May into November.

The warm rains mingle with the cooler rain,

If only she return to me again.

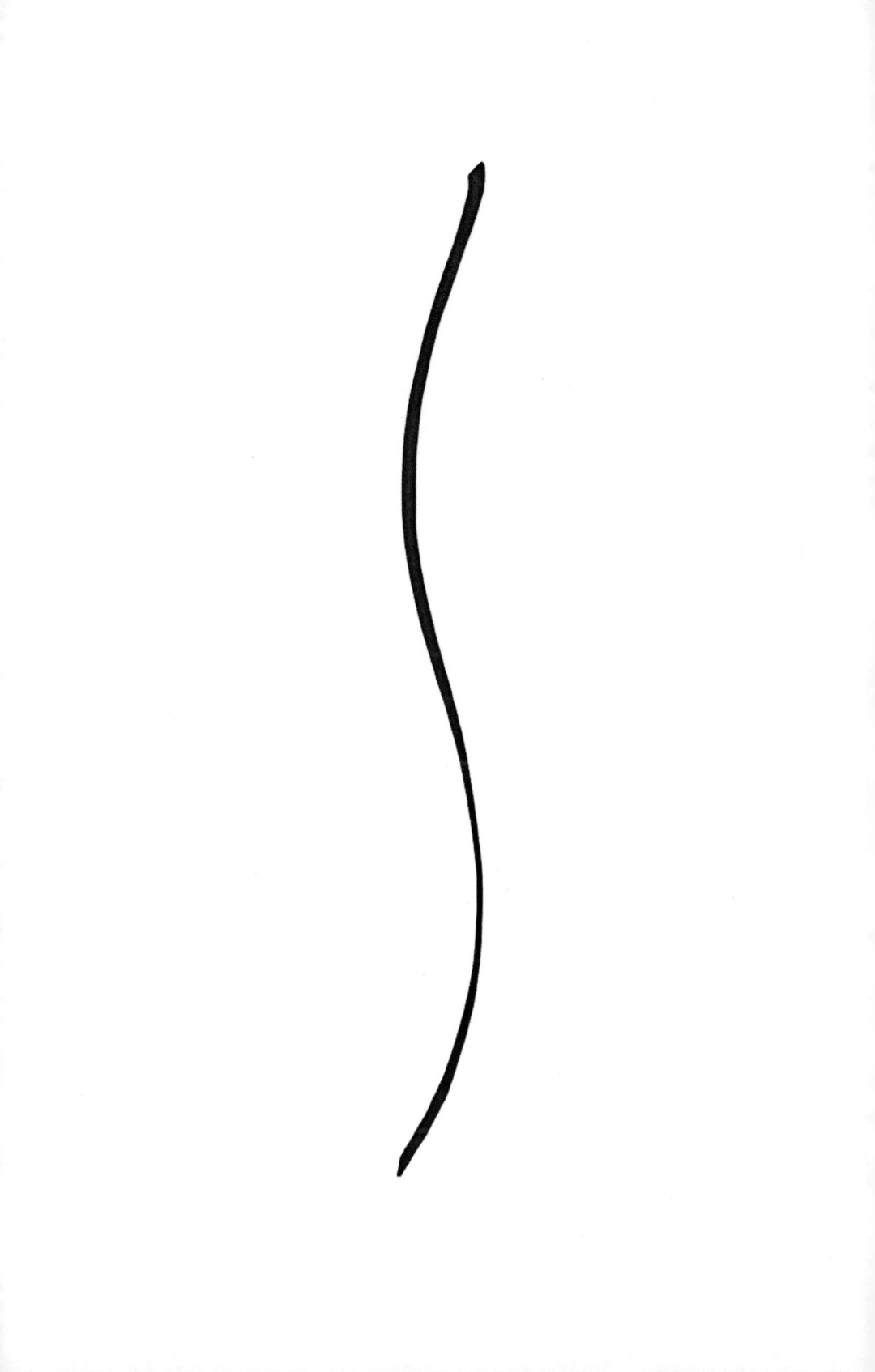

Evening

The skies

Are darker now. My eyes

Dimmer, blind almost. Still

That other eye, wound-red, burning in the west

Stands, stares at me, waits, as the ocean

Rises to swallow it, invincibly.

Elephant clouds, massive, ridged, grey,

Their raw damaged skins dissolving,

Lumber silent across the horizon

To where there must be graveyards,

In the forests of the night.

Immortal ones, what do they care

That villages burn, that my love has fled from me.

Some say there once were white sails, that skimmed along the sea.

Still

Still, only, yes, still

I will pursue her

And she will run and return and run

And never never be mine again

And the sun will shine and the rain will rain

And the grass grow over us unheeding.

Or else, yes, only, still

She will return and the trees will sudden bloom

And we will race hand in hand to the tape,

Be possibly, only, still, a small while happy

And the sun will shine and the rain will rain

And the grass grow over us unheeding.

I cannot cease. Is there another way?

I don my well-worn costume every day.

I know the end. I smile. I act the play.

Change

(Beacon Street, Boston)

Always, always, always, everything changes --

Panta rhei – the single ancient law

Still with us, unrevocable.

I walked this pavement half a life ago,

Thick stately brick enveloping calm

Separate walkers, serene, unhurried,

Saturated in the sureness of their silence.

Now, silence is extinct. The very posts

Flash and burp and stutter their commands.

The walkers, half machines, chatter and scream

Without a pause. They're not alone. A blessing? Yet

Their eyes are up and out. They look past me,

Through me. They are not here. And I?

I walk, as then. She is not here. Again.

I am caught in the beat of the scream of my heart

Where nothing changes ever, ever, ever.

Pompeii, April

One single couple, coupling,

Unheeding, caught

Frozen

In the hot lava flows.

Wherever love blossoms, danger grows.

Brief is the dance of the shimmering May-moth

By the light of the moon.

A happy mortal shall know

His mortality soon.

At the end of her bittersweet ultimate aria

The aging world-renowned soprano

Loses breath.

The orchestra swells, ecstatic, triumphant.

The conductor is death.

Only

In the soft

Unwary

Earth it is

Spring,

And the blades of the grass grow

Up

Through lava,

Through tombs,

Through everything.

Songs are sung. One bird, singing,

Has found another bird.

Ever higher and clearer the lark's serenade

As huge the hawk circles above.

Wherever danger blossoms,

Grows love.

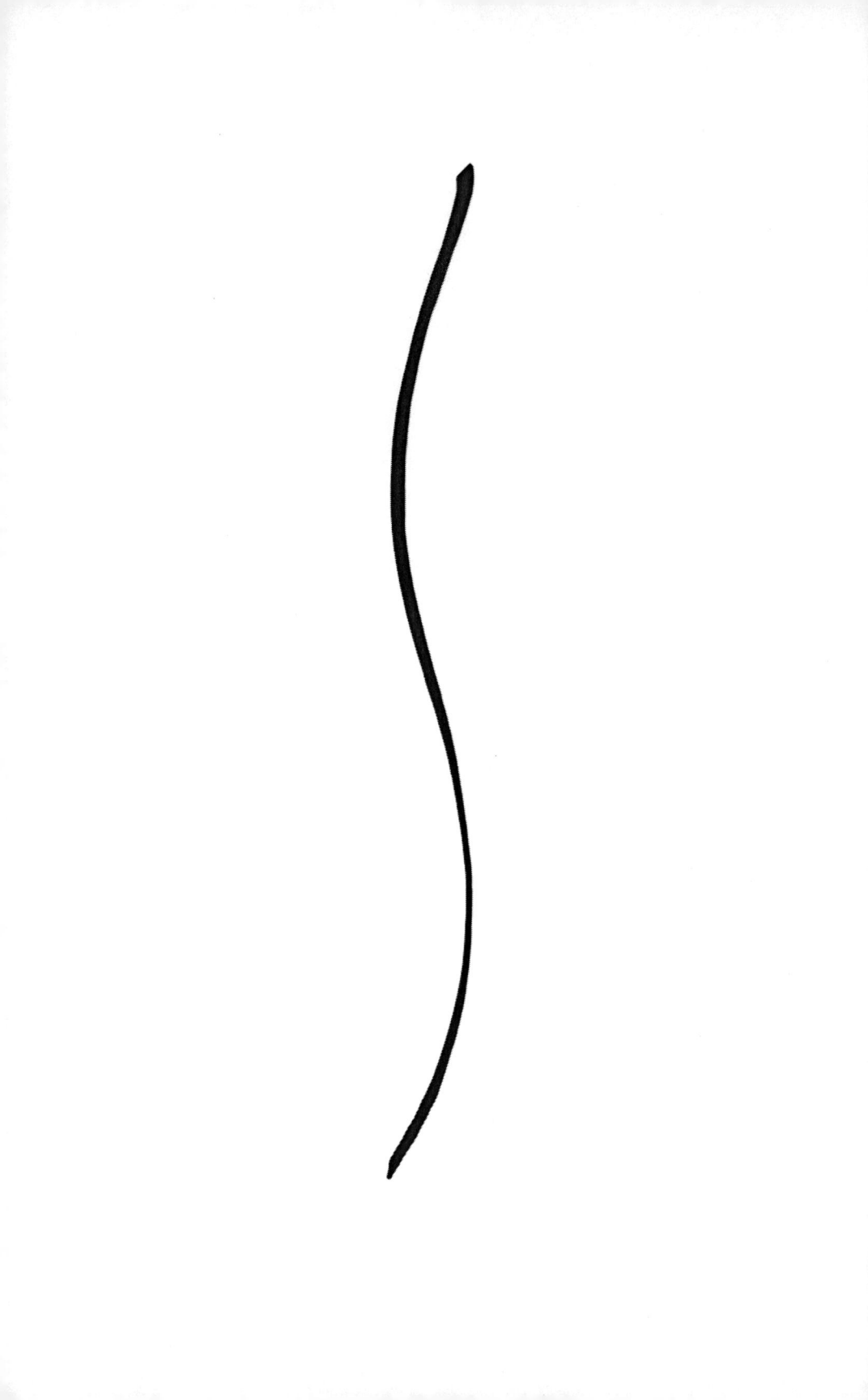

Answer

Tremble, scholar,

There are earthquakes not answers.

The truth you hold within your arms

Is all you will ever hold.

The oldest snowman in the land is but one season old.

Undefended Clouds

The undefended clouds let go

Their only rain.

The West wind's over my mountain pass

And I am come mad again.

Love Is

Love is manufactured by lovers.

And the windmill

In the fury

Of its spinning

Creates the wind.

Blue

The sky is blue. The sky is blue.

The sea is calm. The sky is blue.

The sky is blue. The sky is blue.

Nothing more perfect. The sky is blue.

The sky is blue. The sky is blue.

Still I am here. The sky is blue.

The sky is blue. And you? And you?

The sky is blue. The sky is blue.

Joan

Pure figure, no ground,

All signal, no noise,

Absolute Joan,

Arc flame,

Mad as … no matter

Be mine.

Tiger

I know the tiger. Fro and to and fro

His great limbs pace the tiny barren space.

I see his desperate eyes, hear the ache in his breath.

I know his cry for freedom.

But wait, the keeper comes, bearing great slabs of meat,

And lo, my tiger chews and turns at once

Immeasurably content, totally at peace.

 I know nothing. Nothing. Do I know you

As I know the tiger? I meet, again, again,

The cold iron bars of my cage. I only know

The length, the width, the pain.

The stars of our lives are never

Quite properly aligned.

The tactics of the gods are cruel,

Their strategy neither cruel nor kind.

On the Shore

Evening. I am again here, again,

On this perhaps slightly foreign coast.

A single line of lights, glimmering,

Curves out to the end of the bend of the sky.

Beyond it black. Unknown. From here no doubt

The great ships sailed, laden top-heavy with hope,

Into the dark. She is not here. Again.

I watch, on the terrace of the one café.

Dark. Tempting. Unknowable. I am

Again an old man. I am already a boy.

I have been here twenty times, on twenty seashores

I have never been here. Should anything occur,

There are scores of witnesses.

There is no one but me. There is on this earth

Only one line of lights, one shore, one sea.

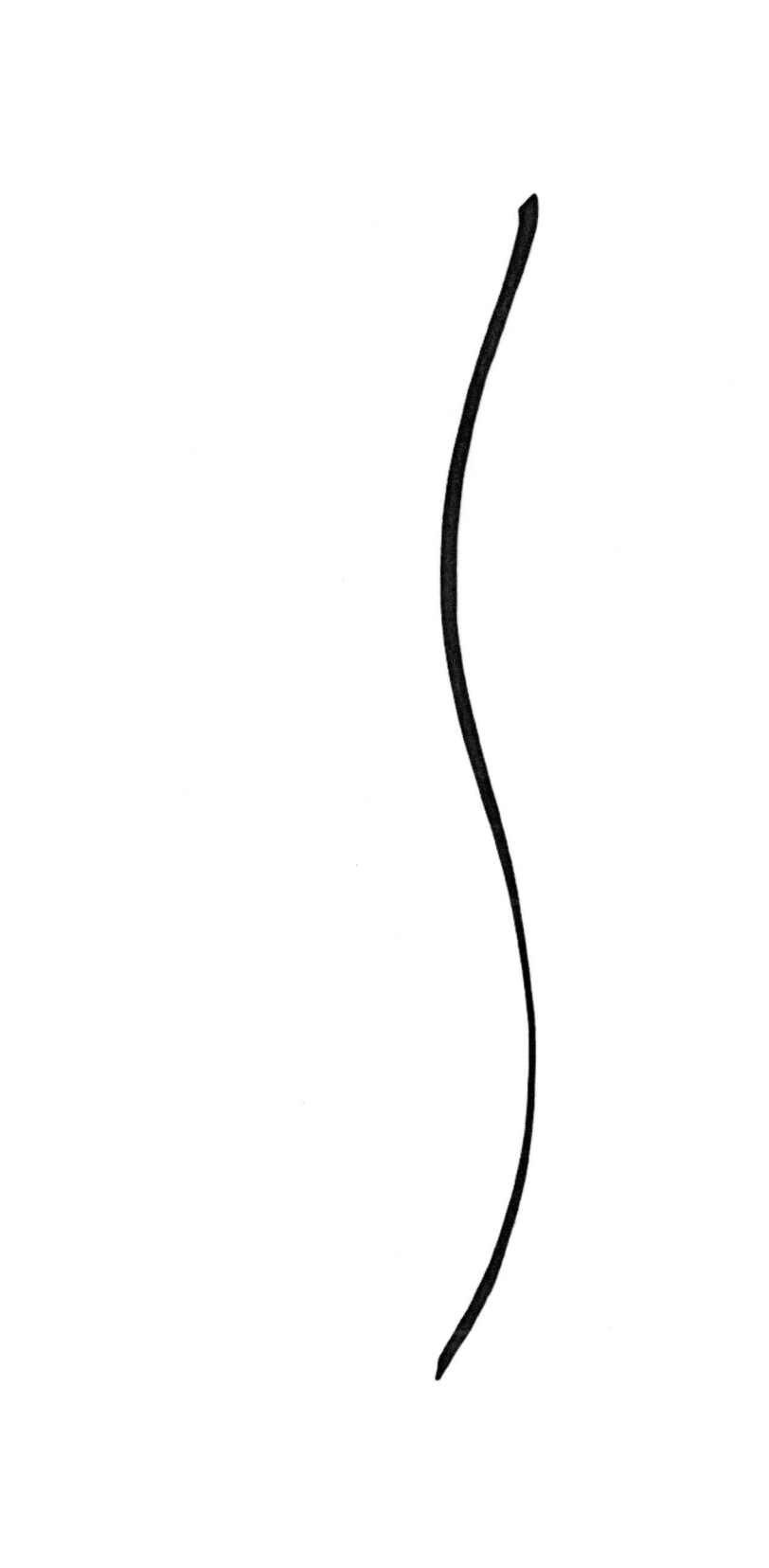

Fools' Gold

Could that be gold there, gleaming among the rocks?

No no, that's fools' gold. Hard to tell. Real gold

Is somehow ... different. Of course some say all gold

Is fools' gold. But that's another tale.

That lovely girl, deep in the forest,

Could that be beauty, half hidden from the eye?

No no, fools' beauty, quite common in these parts.

It can be hard to tell. In fact some say ...

Is this true love I feel, or is it fools' love?

It's hard, sometimes, to tell. Or is all love ...

Some never know it till they die, if then.

Wisdom? Fools' wisdom I suppose. What else

Is there? Give me something I can keep.

Well then, try this. *Cogito ergo sum.*

Cogito – think, can mean I doubt. I doubt

Therefore I am. That's all you need. Don't weep.

There's no fools' doubt. That's something you can hold.

That sparkle in the rocks? It might be gold.

Unicorn

The unicorn is a horny beast.

He feeds delicately, deftly eludes

Pursuit. He lives, at least

In fable.

Yet daily broods,

For in what field, what sunlit glen, what stable,

In what real or what imagined state

Exists his mate?

For Ogden

The poor you shall always have with you, says preacher

While the nouveaux-riches grow nouveaux-richer.

He And She

If Eve lies suncurled catcontent

Who am I to Adam her up,

To name her names,

Set bounds between the allnimals,

Denominate the legal and illegal fruit,

Carve the sharp truth from the luscious enveloping lies.

Mine to name, may I not leave unnamed?

Suppose I do not individuate the serpent,

Suppose

I close

My eyes?

Alcohol Helps

Alcohol helps make fine distinctions:

I am right. You are not.

Simplifies breakups and extinctions.

All good officers drink a lot.

Echoes

The plath to gory

Is the weigh of the whirled

History

Circle moth around flaming son

Woe man's war kiss never done

Babylone crescent Jerusalem's cry

Overdeathermined the role of the die

Lullaby ?

When the reignbough breaks

Cradled rays of the sun king fall

Cumulus queen hangs huge in the sky

In a lightening gash the sword's from the stone

And the prints forever eye

The Evidence of our Senses

A clear fetal heartbeat is frequently heard,

On auscultation by a trained physician,

In a woman who is after all not pregnant.

In textbooks pictures, meticulously drawn,

Depicted homunculi, well known to live in sperm,

As seen in new high-powered microscopes.

We hear what we know, see what we want to see.

Our senses are known for their plasticity.

Wish-fulfillment draws my map.

A twig at the door ? A knock ? Come in!

All the hills have nipples when you leave me,

The dunes are softest skin.

January

Ice is.

Deep down

A slender molecule divides,

Guided precisely by the sightless engineer of love.

Daffodils

Shall

Be.

Soon Enough

Fast as a falling stone

The grey gull

Falls

Into the ash-grey

Sea.

Diving for food,

Or dying,

It will catch a fish

Or be one

Soon enough.

Tonight

Tonight is the night they will castrate the lion.

The rumors scuttle like sudden unhid spiders

To each dank corner where a nest is built for rumors

And settle softly there. The small ones know.

The nurses are afraid. For pay alone not love they stay.

Their slick sunned faces today are as white as their breasts.

Eyes like rubber bound upward and sideways and down.

White starch is soggy somehow.

Tonight is the night they will castrate the lion.

Uniformed also, the green guards pace,

Placed, not without reason, about the room,

Peripheral, for a guard can only be peripheral.

Had one wished to be central he might have been

A king, perhaps, perhaps a king of beasts.

When one is king the rest are always beasts,

Even tonight.

Tonight is the night the young ones say their prayers.

The old insist the young ones say their prayers.

It matters little why, for what, to whom. Only,

The old ones like to see the young ones pray.

It gives a sort of comfort to the old,

Not unlike squashing beetles with the foot,

A necessary comfort sometimes,

When the young have bristly hair and great white teeth

And gleaming yellow eyes.

Tonight, love, there will be a soft moon and no stars,

Only a yellow moon. And silence. And the clouds

Racing by with their great manes flying. Only the clouds

And you and I, padding softly through the dark woods

Stalking our joy.

Nothing else, love. Silence,

And moon and clouds and you and I.

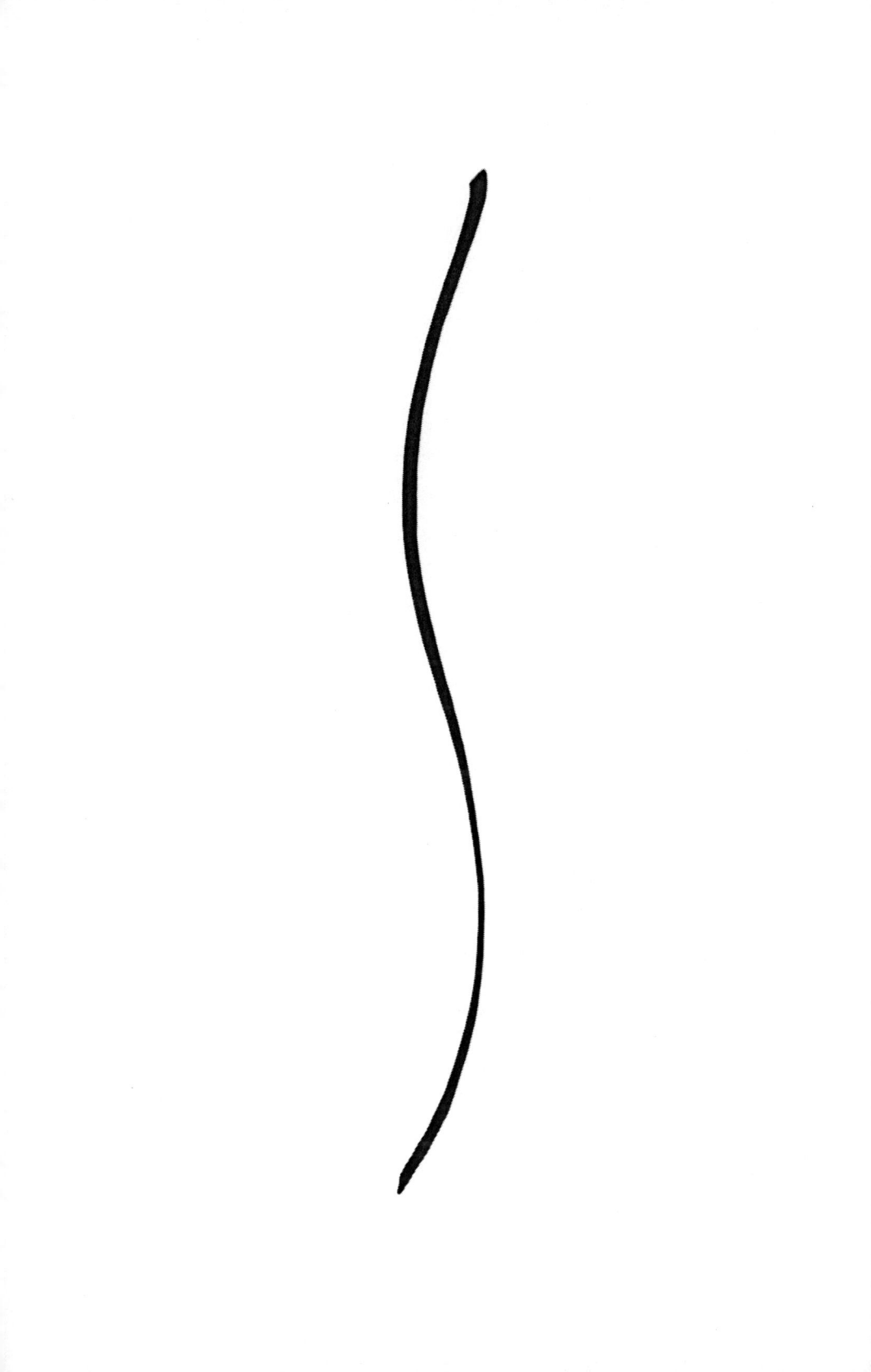

But Eve

A green glass cliff leaps up from the ocean

Where no cliff can possibly be.

Adam has his job,

To set the bounds between the creatures,

Give each a name, and follow father's law.

He does it well. He questions not,

Arises quickly from his dreamless sleep,

Content with his world, his lord content with him.

But Eve

Is not the same.

Given no assignment but to be companion,

She sees his work, and sees he does it well.

All in order, each creature in its place,

Clear, articulate, separate.

But Eve is not so sure. She is a dreamer.

Suppose it were different? She dreams chimeras.

Suppose that this one changed a bit. Suppose

This kind over here could mate with that.

But no! And yet why not? She is a questioner.

She is not tenured in tranquility.

The world is fraught with possibility.

By day she walks obedient at Adam's side,

Couples with him at nightfall. He is content,

Falls rapidly to sleep. But Eve,

The night is hers, she is a dreamer.

She is a questioner. Her boundaries are thin.

She sleeps, and Hypnos, the great serpent of the night

Comes softly, twines himself about her thighs,

And speaks to her his wisdom.

Great serpent? There is no such beast,

Adam assures her in the morning light.

I have my catalogue with all the names.

Great serpent? Ha, you must have dreamt

Of my organ here, and lengthened it a bit!

Ho ho ho, he goes off laughing

Across his well-delineated fields.

She looks. The world is bright and clear. He's right,

There are no serpents in the morning light.

But at night the serpent of her dreaming

Continues, and how can she not listen.

She builds not walls as Adam does.

She cannot keep things out, she is a dreamer,

She is a supposer. The insidious serpent

Conjures pictures for her. She sees, she imagines.

I dreamt, she says to Adam, that your creatures changed

One into another. I saw a creature

Part man, part hornéd bull, dangerous it looked,

It frightened me. Yes I can see it still.

And I saw one of those great furry apes

Change slowly and become a man like you!

No no, that is a terrible mad idea,

Such dreams are dangerous, they cannot be.

He takes her firmly across his knee,

Pinkens her bottom. She does not object.

Nor does she cease her dreaming.

But he is troubled. Let us ask our father,

He says at last. And do they go to him for counsel,

And does he give them prohibitions, right and wrong,

And black and white, and do they bite,

And does he hurl them out

Into our bloody separate languages and lands?

Or does he hear a note or two of Hypnos,

Is this my creature too, is this again my voice?

And does he offer them solace. You may think

And you may dream. You need not be as one.

And do they continue making borders, dreaming?

And am I yet an actor in their play?

Am I the creature of his planful naming?

Am I the creature of her dreams?

The glass cliff gleams.

It speaks to me no words, no meaning.

The cliff is what I see.

Warrior

Achilles died at so they say nineteen.

Ridiculous! No way that could have been.

Ten years of war, the battles lost and won,

Travels, arguments, triumphs, treacheries.

The man who told you that must have been far gone.

No, not a tale, a thing I've somehow seen…

I am a dreamer. Perhaps it was a dream.

Achilles died at so they say nineteen?

The purest of sculptors works only in ice in the summer.

There was one, I knew him, Ikalos was his name.

Innocent of the dust of museums, innocent of fame,

His work was not by mortal man resistible.

Here's how he worked. His students cut for him

At night a block of ice from the deepest caves,

And raised it to his workshop by the road.

He carved all night, his followers about him.

By morning a new creation had emerged.

Word spread. Shops closed. They came from everywhere

To gaze. Sausages were sold, frail children sometimes crushed.

At noon the sculpture's tears began to mar its shape.

By night it had relaxed into its simpler state.

He carved, I have seen it, a god by the roadside,

A great bearded deity that caught each traveler that tried to pass

And held him all the morning by his gaze.

Soon grew a densening throng of chanting worshippers

Until their god turned puddle at mid-afternoon,

And they woke from their belief with a tear in their eye.

Even now they wonder. They are not as once they were.

He formed his ice into a maiden once

To cure a certain overesthetic prince

Who was impotent, sad, cared for no one, loved

His books alone. As Ikalos built the girl

Each man who watched fell hopelessly in love

And would have leapt upon her but the prince was first.

The embracing ice so heated him he lost

His sense, his fluids, his illness all at once

As she warmed in his embrace, became his tears.

The prince became … not happy, but more liked.

Yet hear me, these were but his early works

That he scarce would have remembered.

His final piece, few saw it, was a warrior of ice,

For an instant so perfect it put the gods to shame.

Apollo some say was furious and increased

The strength and heat of his great flaming orb

To boiling point. And Zeus they say , furious as well,

Hurled his lightning down to that same place.

I heard all art was outlawed for a time.

Ah, but for that brief hour the warrior shone,

I saw him but a moment (I was then young.

I am no longer young.) I see him still.

The warrior grew. I swear that we could see

Flesh and metal, earth and air and fire

Made from his single watery element.

Tall and straight yet somehow soft, the youth

Was also part a woman, part in tears. A fierce

Man of power and still a trusting child.

I saw beauty bare and wanted nothing, only to die.

I felt the soft down on his golden skin, smelled lilacs

In his hair, tasted the sweat upon his lip. and heard

His sword drawn from the scabbard. Saw it held high,

As it drew up the total glorious body, our gaze,

And the shining earth itself. Higher and higher,

I saw it catch the sun on its weeping point

(Was it the gods?) and gleam and burst entire into flame,

And gone. But I have seen what I have seen.

Achilles died at so they say nineteen.

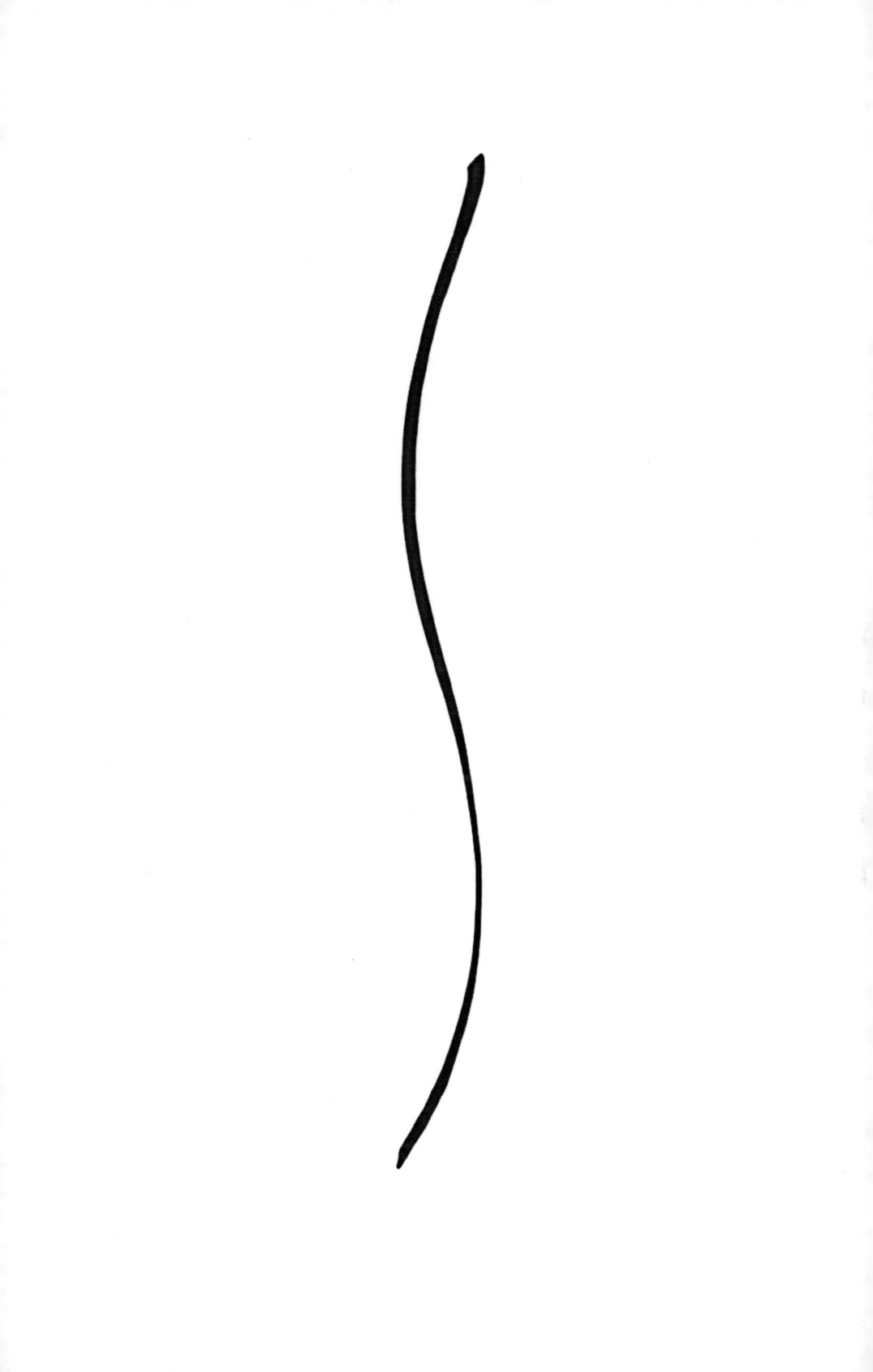

Eyes

The Queen

Fuck the queen. She is yours. We are yours.

Free our blind city, far-sighted one,

Fresh back from foreign lands you thought your own.

Exercise your dreams on our sunlit streets.

Answer the riddle the great monster asks.

Break the spell! Fill the throne! Fuck the queen!

The Riddle

First the riddle:

Give only the single answer that is in you to give

To whatever question comes.

Four legs, two legs, three legs?

Man.

Two stone, twelve stone, one stone?

Man.

Two eyes, a thousand eyes, no eyes?

Man.

In your mirror is your reply.

Whatever monster-question is released,

But let your answer loose to mate with it,

And conquer on.

Is it not Convenient?

The city is yours, the queen is yours.

The stars walk with you, and some say the sun.

Not all men envy you their light,

It could be damning were there aught to hide.

Is it not convenient

That the king was already dead,

Died even as you came.

A kingéd city is not quite so kind

To passing heroes. Ours, open, called aloud to you

To be her master. Is it not convenient?

I have known few men allowed such fortune,

And those few are not living men.

Far-sighted One

Your eyes

Are eyes beloved of the gods.

You see matters that we cannot see.

From afar you saw our plight,

And what our troubled queen, still lovely, wished you saw.

Never has the queen been so radiant, so young.

Some say we need no longer send our boys

As messengers across the distant hills

To Delphi, for your eyes can see as well.

You see the death of our late king

And that the death must be avenged, though you cannot yet see

The murderer. It is far-sighted you are, Oedipus, exceeding far.

The Hunt

My feet were swollen, pus-filled, yet I played

With all the shining princes of that land.

Their sports not mine I played and always I was the victor,

Except the races -- that was hardest -- and at first the hunt.

Even in hunting I lusted to be first,

Spent hours quiet, watching in the forest,

Spying every movement in the distant green.

My eyes grew keen at last and overcame their speed:

I knew precisely where to run and when to kill.

This was my finest victory, the hunt.

The Old Man

Remember the old man,

Thick, swart, gnarled as the ancient olive,

Planted, still, at the center of the crossroads,

Stubborn as yourself,

More stubborn, possibly, he remains there still.

His will was too much kindred to your own.

You might have paused; if not his face, his years.

Your sword alas was longer than your tears.

Yet time is also long,

And there will be a time for weeping.

Remember the old man.

The Plague

The plague is rampant. Our king must be avenged.

Messengers they say are drawing closer.

The queen's eye is overcast as it has not been

Since the day she cast away her only son.

Have you not noticed? No, you have not noticed.

You are occupied in your glorious hunt, in searching

The vast distant plains.

Far and wide range the eyes of great Oedipus.

Near and narrow the pathways of the gods.

The Professor

Why, Oedipus, are you of a sudden become teacher?

You preach to us your people virtues that we know of;

Honor the dead; honor thy father, thy mother love;

Keep family joined. Sober thoughts, yet you speak

Drunken, wild-eyed, rapid, as thought you felt the schoolhouse tremble

And feared a quake would interrupt your speech.

Is our destruction now within your sight?

The Reflection

Already messengers are approaching through the storm.

There is not much time. The prey is sighted. Sound your horn.

Dream the dreams that after all mean nothing,

A man may lie with any in his dreams.

There is no fault except as in the earth

At certain lines that draw the earthquake in.

Revere your mother and father. Conquer the city.

Remember your answer. In your mirror is your reply.

Beware, the lightning makes a glass of every puddle.

Kill only strangers, remember.

Fuck the queen. A man may lie. Remember the old man.

Look harder, look farther with your eagle eye

And keep your talons ready for the city's defiler.

Look always forward, do not pause,

Do not look down, there's danger all about you,

Madness or death in ceasing to follow the gods' command.

There is a messenger approaching.

The lightning flash is knowledge. Darkness is my prize.

A queen may lie with any man. The oracle never lies.

In a pool of water I have seen the old man's eyes.

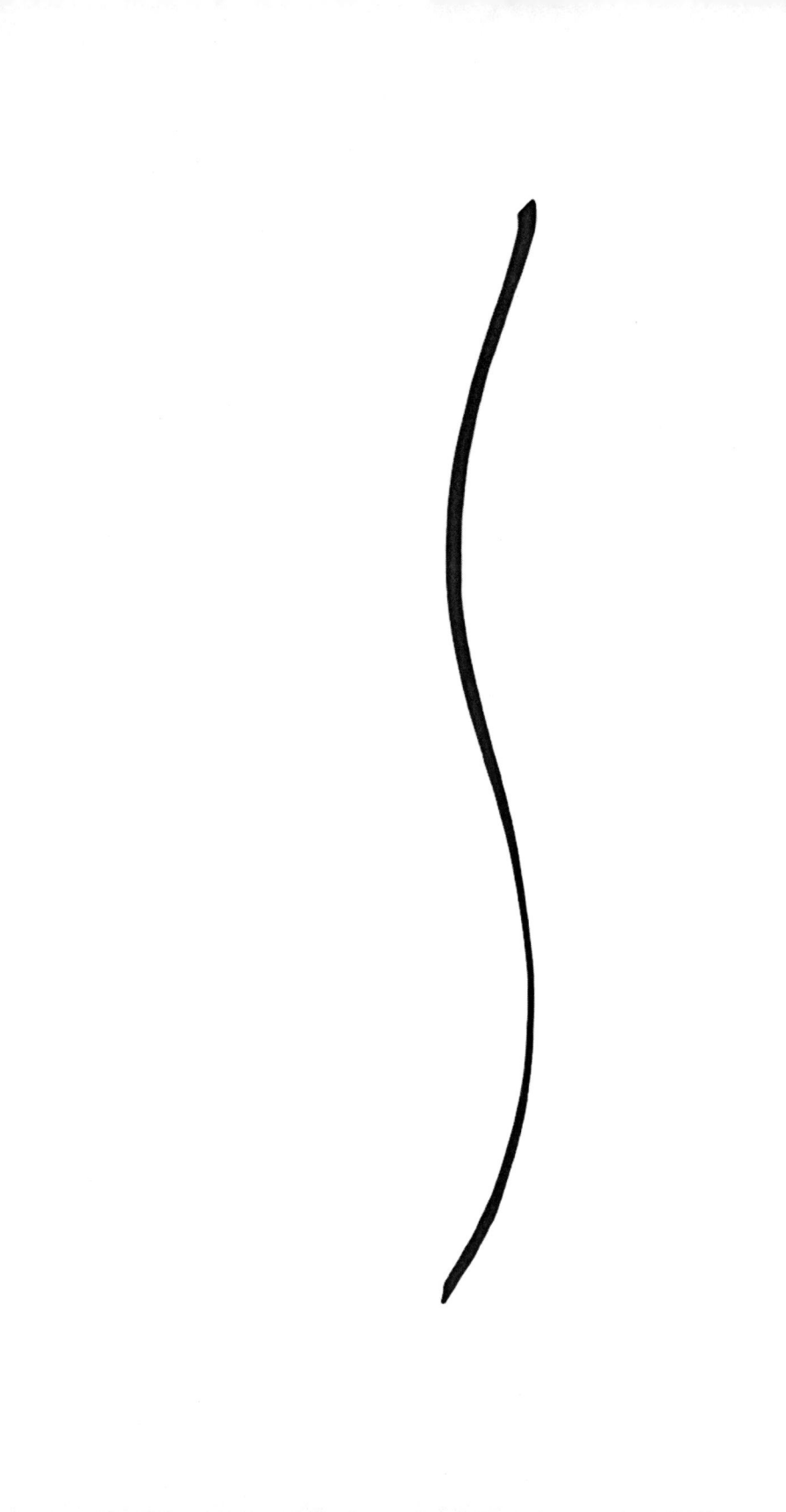

Arlington 1963

He lies,

They stand,

And guard him, stiff as bright toy soldiers.

The grass is green. The music plays.

It must be a game.

The grass is gone.

The hill is pasted thick with faces,

Coats and faces, black and white and blurred.

An old newsreel perhaps. Someone will come and explain.

The music is gone.

He lies.

I stand

Stiff, and salute, and half unwilling draw my breath.

A leaden-hearted old toy soldier

Before the idiot majesty of death.

CPSIA information can be obtained at www.ICGtesting.com
229036LV00001B/3/P

9 781614 342229